PIANO VOCAL GUITAR

HAL•LEONARD
ESSENTIAL SONGS

The 1950s

W9-CPF-597

ISBN 0-634-09104-2

HAL•LEONARD®
CORPORATION
7777 W. BLUEMOUND RD. P.O. BOX 13819 MILWAUKEE, WI 53213

Visit Hal Leonard Online at
www.halleonard.com

CONTENTS

203	Long Tall Sally	Little Richard	6	1956
206	Love and Marriage	Dinah Shore/Frank Sinatra	20/5	1955
212	Love Me Tender	Elvis Presley	1	1956
214	A Lover's Question	Clyde McPhatter	6	1959
218	Loving You	Elvis Presley	20	1957
209	Magic Moments	Perry Como	4	1958
220	(You've Got) The Magic Touch	The Platters	4	1956
226	Memories Are Made of This	Dean Martin/Gale Storm	1/5	1956
223	Mister Sandman	The Chordettes/Four Aces	1/5	1954/55
232	Moments to Remember	The Four Lads	2	1955
235	Mona Lisa	Nat King Cole/Victor Young/Harry James	1/7/14	1950
238	(Put Another Nickel In) Music! Music! Music!	Teresa Brewer/The Ames Brothers/Hugo Winterhalter	1/14/17	1950
240	My Heart Cries for You	Guy Mitchell/Dinah Shore/Vic Damone	2/3/4	1951
242	My Heart Is an Open Book	Carl Dobkins, Jr.	3	1959
248	My Prayer	The Platters	1	1956
252	Never Be Anyone Else But You	Ricky Nelson	6	1959
245	Oh, Lonesome Me	Don Gibson	7	1958
256	Oh! My Pa-Pa (O Mein Papa)	Eddie Fisher/Eddie Calvert	1/6	1954
260	Papa Loves Mambo	Perry Como	4	1954
265	Party Doll	Buddy Knox/Steve Lawrence	1/5	1957
268	(You've Got) Personality	Lloyd Price	2	1959
274	Poor Little Fool	Ricky Nelson	1	1958
276	Primrose Lane	Jerry Wallace	8	1959
271	Put Your Head on My Shoulder	Paul Anka	2	1959
278	Rock Around the Clock	Bill Haley & His Comets	1	1955
280	Sea of Love	Phil Phillips with The Twilights	2	1959
284	Searchin'	The Coasters	3	1957
288	See Saw	Don Cornell/The Moonglows	57/25	1956
293	See You Later, Alligator	Bill Haley & His Comets	6	1956
296	Since I Don't Have You	The Skyliners	12	1959
301	Sincerely	McGuire Sisters/Moonglows	1/20	1955
304	Singing the Blues	Guy Mitchell	1	1956
310	Sixteen Candles	The Crests	2	1959
312	Sixteen Tons	Tennessee Ernie Ford	1	1955
307	Smoke Gets in Your Eyes	The Platters	1	1959
314	Stagger Lee	Lloyd Price	1	1959
320	The Stroll	The Diamonds	4	1958
324	Tammy	Debbie Reynolds/The Ames Brothers	1/5	1957
317	Teach Me Tonight	Jo Stafford/Dianna Washington	15/23	1954
326	Tears on My Pillow	Little Anthony & The Imperials	4	1958
329	(Let Me Be Your) Teddy Bear	Elvis Presley	1	1957
332	Tennessee Waltz	Patti Page/Les Paul & Mary Ford/Jo Stafford	1/6/7	1950/51/51
335	Tequila	Champs/Eddie Platt	1/20	1958
338	That's Amoré (That's Love)	Dean Martin	2	1953
343	There Goes My Baby	The Drifters	2	1959
348	Tom Dooley	Kingston Trio	1	1958
350	Tonight You Belong to Me	Patience and Prudence	4	1956
353	True Love	Bing Crosby & Grace Kelly	3	1956
356	Turn Me Loose	Fabian	9	1959
362	Twilight Time	The Platters	1	1958
359	The Walk	Jimmy McCracklin	7	1958
364	The Wayward Wind	Gogi Grant	1	1956
367	Wear My Ring Around Your Neck	Elvis Presley	2	1958
370	What'd I Say	Ray Charles	6	1959
374	A White Sport Coat (And a Pink Carnation)	Marty Robbins	1	1957
377	Why	Frankie Avalon	1	1959
380	Why Don't You Believe Me	Joni James/Patti Page	1/4	1952/53
390	Wonderful! Wonderful!	Johnny Mathis	14	1957
382	You Belong to Me	Jo Stafford/Patti Page/Dean Martin	1/1/12	1952
386	Young Blood	The Coasters	8	1957

ALL SHOOK UP

Words and Music by OTIS BLACKWELL
and ELVIS PRESLEY

AT THE HOP

Words and Music by ARTHUR SINGER,
JOHN MADARA and DAVID WHITE

ALONG CAME JONES

Words and Music by JERRY LEIBER
and MIKE STOLLER

chas - in' poor Sweet Sue.
time that I got back.
same old ro - de - o.

He trapped her in the old___
Down in the old a - ban -
Sal - ty Sam was a -

___ saw mill and said with an e - vil laugh:___
doned mine Sweet Sue was - a hav - in' fits.___
try'n' to stuff Sweet Sue in a bur - lap sack.___

(Spoken): "If
(Spoken): That
(Spoken): He said, "If

you don't gim - me the deed___ to your ranch I'll saw you all in
vil - lian said, "Gim - me the deed___ to your ranch or I'll blow you all to
you don't gim - me the deed___ to your ranch I'm gon - na throw you on the rail - road

D°7

freely

half."
bits."
track."

And then he grabbed her.
And then he grabbed her.
And then he grabbed her.

And then? He
And then? He
And then? He

Repeat bars for 3rd verse only

tied her up. And then? He turned on the buzz-saw. And
tied her up. And then? He lit the fuse to the dynamite. And
tied her up. And then? He threw her on the railroad track. And
then? A train started coming. And

then? And then? And then a-

a tempo
tacet

A♭ 4fr.

long came— Jones,———

E♭7

tall thin— Jones;———

ARE YOU SINCERE

Words and Music by WAYNE WALKER
and LUCKY MOELLER

AUTUMN LEAVES

English lyric by JOHNNY MERCER
French lyric by JACQUES PREVERT
Music by JOSEPH KOSMA

21

THE BIG HURT

Words and Music by
WAYNE SHANKLIN

BE-BOP-A-LULA

Words and Music by TEX DAVIS
and GENE VINCENT

Moderately slow Rock

Be-bop-a-lu-la, she's my ba-by. Be-bop-a-lu-la, I don't mean may-be.

Be-bop-a-lu-la, she's my ba-by. Be-bop-a-lu-la, I don't mean may-be.

Be-bop-a-lu-la, she's my ba-by doll, my ba-by doll, my ba-by doll.

BELIEVE WHAT YOU SAY

Words and Music by DORSEY BURNETTE
and JOHNNY BURNETTE

BIRD DOG

Words and Music by
BOUDLEAUX BRYANT

VERSE

Johnny is a joker *Spoken:* (He's a bird) A very funny joker

(He's a bird) But when he jokes my honey (He's a dog) His

jokin' ain't so funny (What a dog) Johnny is the joker that's a-

Hey, bird dog, you'd bet-ter get a-way quick.__ Bird dog, you'd bet-ter find a chick-en lit-tle of your own.__

own.__

VERSE

2. Johnny sings a love song *(Like a bird)*
He sings the sweetest love song *(You ever heard)*
But when he sings to my gal *(What a howl)*
To me he's just a wolf dog *(On the prowl)*
Johnny wants to fly away and puppy love my baby *(He's a bird dog)*
(CHORUS)

3. Johnny kissed the teacher *(He's a bird)*
He tiptoed up to reach her *(He's a bird)*
Well, he's the teacher's pet now *(He's a dog)*
What he wants he can get now *(What a dog)*
He even made the teacher let him sit next to my baby. *(He's a bird dog)*
(CHORUS)

BLUEBERRY HILL

Words and Music by AL LEWIS,
LARRY STOCK and VINCENT ROSE

BLUE HAWAII
from the Paramount Picture WAIKIKI WEDDING

Words and Music by LEO ROBIN
and RALPH RAINGER

BONY MORONIE

Words and Music by
LARRY WILLIAMS

BREATHLESS

Words and Music by
OTIS BLACKWELL

Bright Rock Tempo

Now, if you love me, let's please don't tease. If I can hold you then
shake all o-ver and you know why. I'm sure it's love and

let me squeeze.
that's no lie.

My heart goes 'round and 'round;
'Cause when you call my name,

my love comes
I burn like

tum - blin' down.
wood in-flamed.

You leave me (breathe out ....)

BORN TO BE WITH YOU

Words and Music by
DON ROBERTSON

BYE BYE LOVE

Words and Music by FELICE BRYANT
and BOUDLEAUX BRYANT

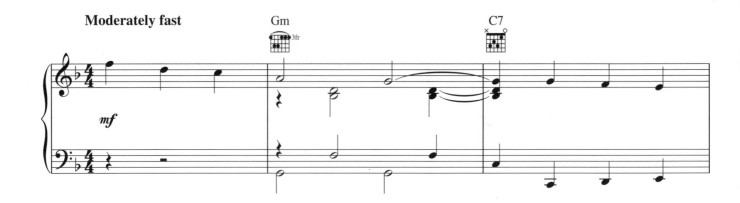

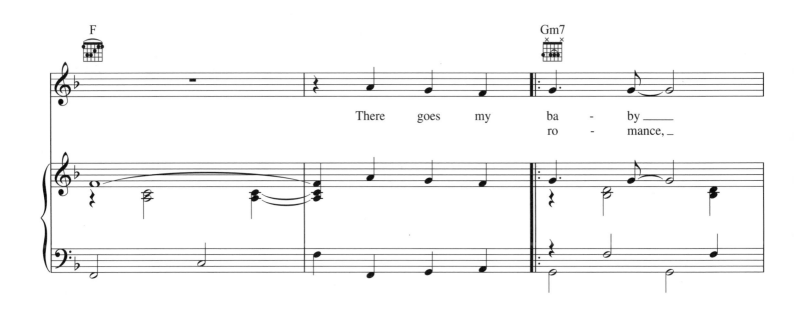

There goes my ba - by ____
ro - mance, ____

with some - one new. _____ She sure looks
I'm through with love. _____ I'm through with

CATCH A FALLING STAR

Words and Music by PAUL VANCE
and LEE POCKRISS

CHANGING PARTNERS

Words by JOE DARION
Music by LARRY COLEMAN

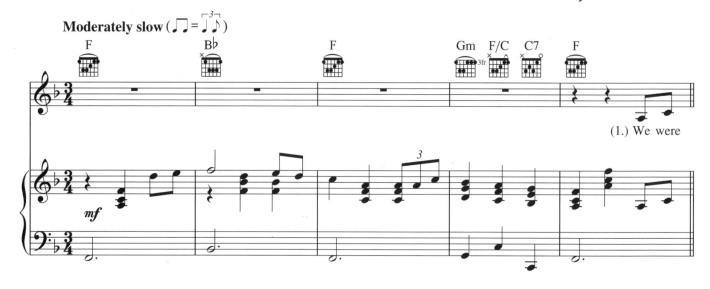

(1.) We were

waltz-in' to-geth-er ___ to a dream-y mel-o-dy, when they
(2., D.S.) danced for one mo-ment, ___ and too soon we had to part, in that

called out change part-ners ___ and you waltzed a-way ___ from
won-der-ful mo-ment, ___ some-thing hap-pened to ___ my

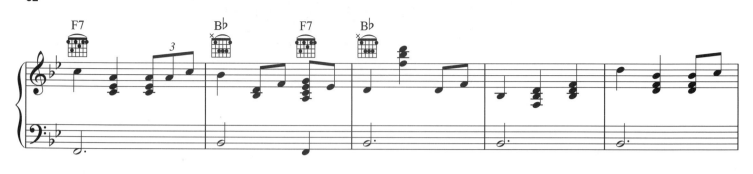

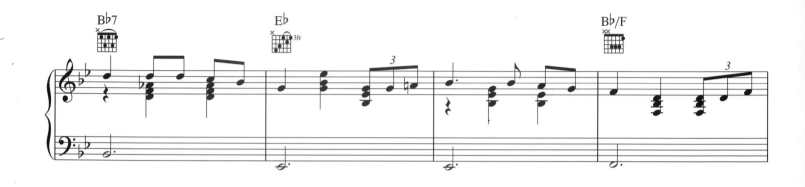

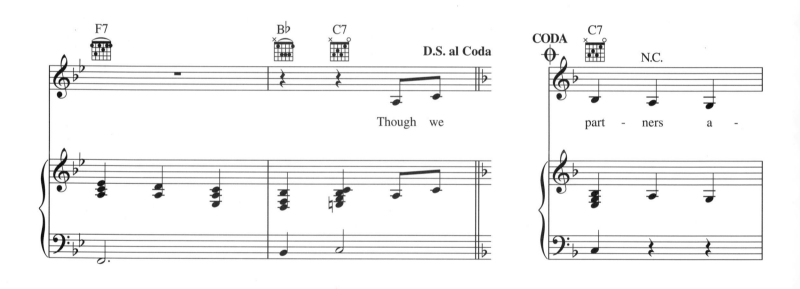

Though we

part - ners a -

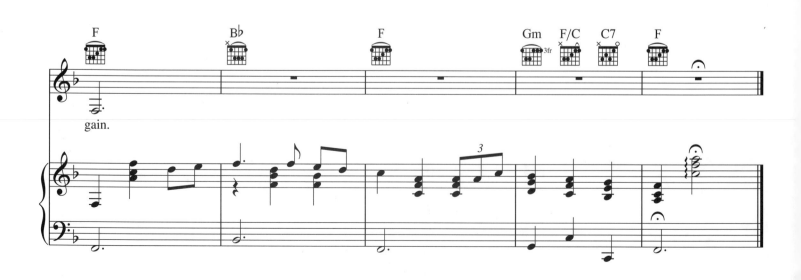

gain.

CHANSON D'AMOUR
(The Ra-Da-Da-Da-Da Song)

Words and Music by
WAYNE SHANKLIN

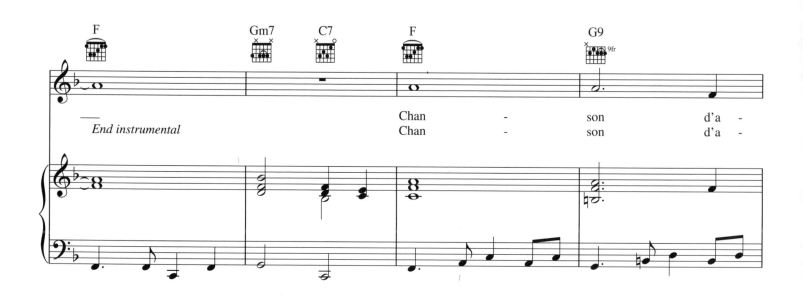

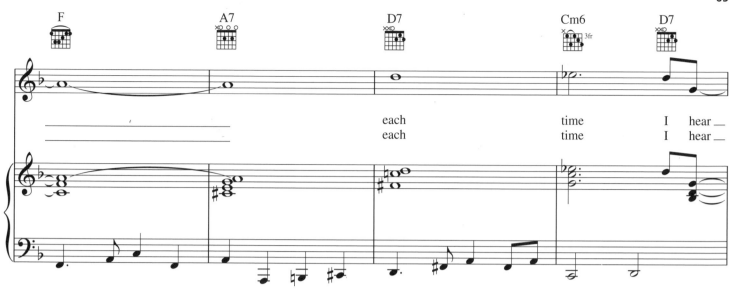

each time I hear ____
each time I hear ____

ra da da da da, chan - son ____ d'a - mour. ____
ra da da da da, chan - son ____ d'a - mour. ____

CHANTILLY LACE

Moderate Boogie Woogie

Words and Music by
J.P. RICHARDSON

CINCO ROBLES
(Five Oaks)

Words by LARRY SULLIVAN
Music by DOROTHY WRIGHT

Moderate waltz

DANCE WITH ME HENRY
(The Wallflower)

Words and Music by HANK BALLARD,
ETTA JAMES and JOHNNY OTIS

Hey, ba - by, what do I have to do ___ to

make you love me too? ___ You got to roll with me, Henry.
Roll with me, Hen - ry. } (Al -

-right, ba - by) Roll ___ with me, Hen - ry. (Don't ___ mean may - be)

THE DAY THE RAINS CAME

English Lyric by CARL SIGMAN
French Lyric by PIERRE DELANOE
Music by GILBERT BECAUD

The day that the rains came down, moth-er earth smiled a-gain. Now the li-lacs could bloom; now the fields could grow green-er. The day that the rains came down, buds were born; love was born.

DIANA

Words and Music by
PAUL ANKA

I'm so young and you're so old. This my dar-ling I've been told. I don't care just what they say 'cause for-ev-er I will pray you and I will be as free as the birds up in the trees. Oh please stay by

DO YOU WANT TO DANCE?

Words and Music by
BOBBY FREEMAN

DON'T

Words and Music by JERRY LEIBER
and MIKE STOLLER

Don't, don't, that's what you
Don't, don't leave what my em-

say, each time that I hold you this way.
brace, for here in my arms is your place.

When I feel like this and I want to kiss you, ba-by, don't say
When the night grows cold and I want to hold you, ba-by, don't say

DON'T BE CRUEL
(To a Heart That's True)

Words and Music by OTIS BLACKWELL
and ELVIS PRESLEY

DON'T YOU KNOW?

Words and Music by
BOBBY WORTH

EARTH ANGEL

Words and Music by
JESSE BELVIN

Slowly with a beat

Earth an - gel, earth an - gel, Will you be mine,— My dar - ling, dear,—

Love you all the time.— I'm just a fool,— A fool in love with

you.— Earth an - gel, earth an - gel,

FEVER

Words and Music by JOHN DAVENPORT
and EDDIE COOLEY

Moderate Jump beat
snap fingers

1. Nev - er know how much I love you, Nev - er know how much I
2. Sun lights up the day - time, Moon lights up the

care. When you put your arms a - round me, I get a
night. I light up when you call my name, And you

fe - ver that's so hard to bear. You give me fe - ver
know I'm gon - na treat you right. }

Verse 3 Romeo loved Juliet
Juliet she felt the same,
When he put his arms around her, he said,
"Julie, baby you're my flame."

Chorus Thou givest fever, when we kisseth
Fever with my flaming youth,
Fever – I'm afire
Fever, yea I burn forsooth.

Verse 4 Captain Smith and Pocahantas
Had a very mad affair,
When her Daddy tried to kill him, she said,
"Daddy-o don't you dare."

Chorus Give me fever, with his kisses,
Fever when he holds me tight.
Fever – I'm his Missus
Oh Daddy won't you treat him right.

Verse 5 Now you've listened to my story
Here's the point that I have made:
Chicks were born to give you fever
Be it fahrenheit or centigrade.

Chorus They give you fever when you kiss them,
Fever if you live and learn.
Fever – till you sizzle
What a lovely way to burn.

EDDIE MY LOVE

Words and Music by AARON COLLINS,
MAXWELL DAVIS and SAUL SAM LING

(Now and Then There's)
A FOOL SUCH AS I

Words and Music by
BILL TRADER

FRIENDLY PERSUASION

Words by PAUL FRANCIS WEBSTER
Music by DIMITRI TIOMKIN

GREAT BALLS OF FIRE

Words and Music by OTIS BLACKWELL
and JACK HAMMER

GUITAR BOOGIE SHUFFLE

By ARTHUR SMITH

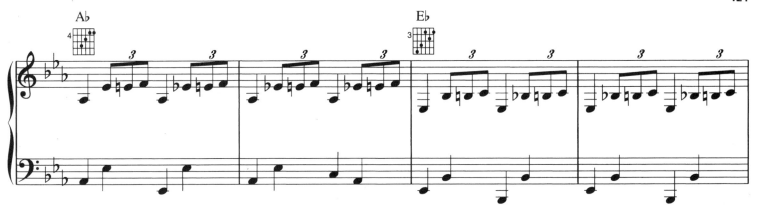

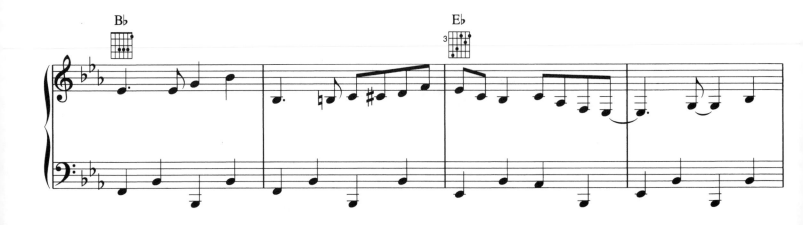

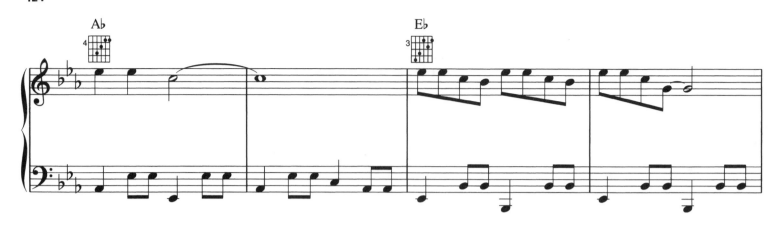

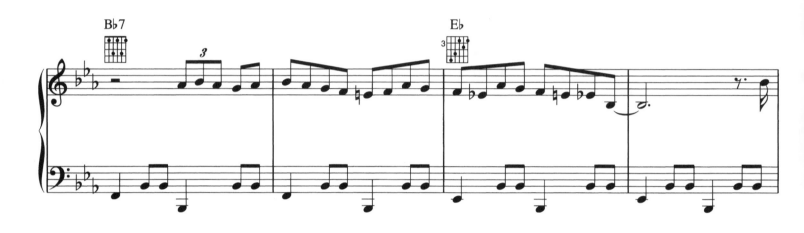

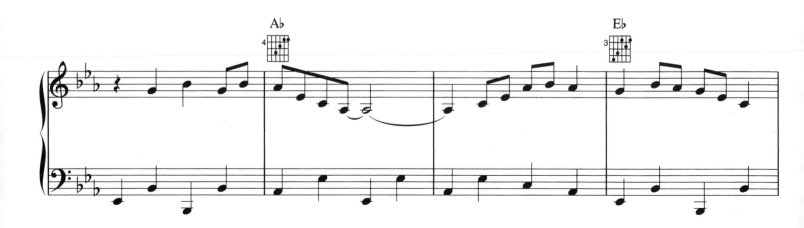

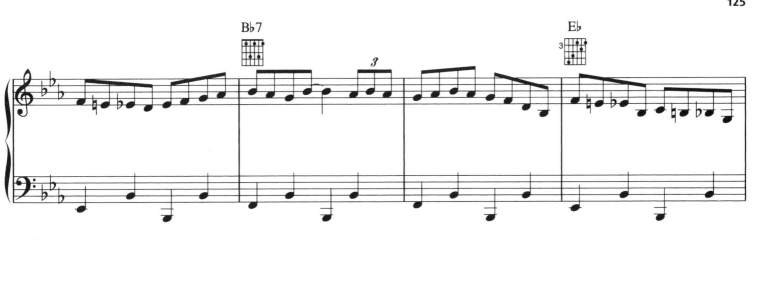

THE GREEN DOOR

Words and Music by BOB DAVIE
and MARVIN MOORE

Moderate tempo

Mid - night ___ one more night with - out sleep - in', _____
Knocked once ___ tried more to tell 'em I'd been there, _____

Watch - ing ___ till the morn - ing comes peep - in', _____
Door slammed ___ hos - pi - tal - i - ty's thin there, _____

Green door ___ what's the se - cret you're keep - in'. _____
Won - der ___ just what's go - in' on in there. _____

THE HAWAIIAN WEDDING SONG
(Ke Kali Nei Au)

English Lyrics by AL HOFFMAN and DICK MANNING
Hawaiian Lyrics and Music by CHARLES E. KING

Slowly, with much warmth

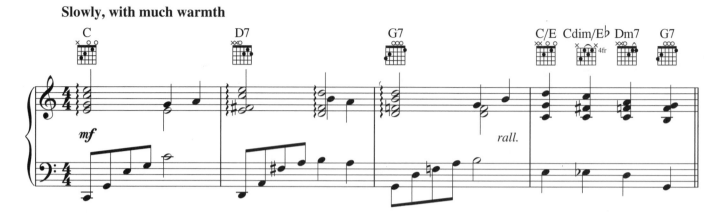

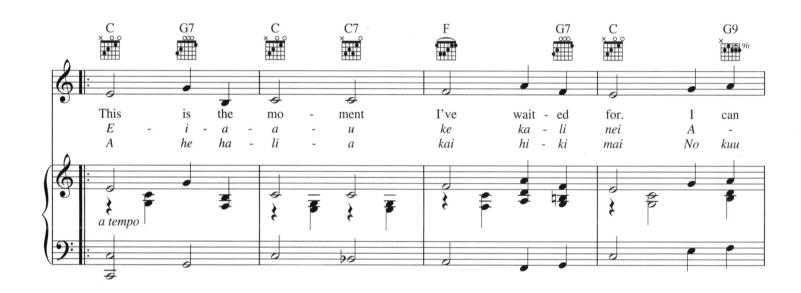

This is the mo - ment I've wait - ed for. I can
E - i - a - a - u ke ka - li nei A -
A he ha - li - a kai hi - ki mai No kuu

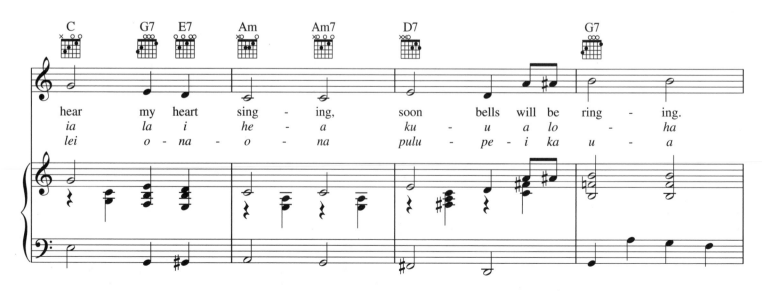

hear my heart sing - ing, soon bells will be ring - ing.
ia la i he - a ku - u a lo - ha
lei o - na - o - na pulu - pe - i ka u - a

HEARTBREAK HOTEL

Words and Music by MAE BOREN AXTON,
TOMMY DURDEN and ELVIS PRESLEY

though it's al - ways crowd-ed, you still can find _ some room for bro-ken-heart - ed lov - ers _ to

cry a - way _ their gloom. _ They'll be so, they'll be just so lone - ly, ba - by,

they'll be just so lone - ly, they'll be so lone - ly _ they could die. Now the

bell - hop's tears keep flow - ing; the desk clerk's _ dressed in black. Well, they've

Heart - break Ho - tel where you will be, will be just so lone - ly, ba - by,

well, you'll be lone - ly. You'll be so lone - ly____ you could die.

A9

Piano solo ad lib.

HEARTACHES BY THE NUMBER

Words and Music by
HARLAN HOWARD

HONEYCOMB

Words and Music by
BOB MERRILL

140

Additional Lyrics

2. Now have you heard tell how they made a bee?
Then tried a hand at a green, green tree.
So the tree was made and I guess you've heard,
Next they made a bird.
Then they went around lookin' everywhere,
Takin' love from here and from there,
And they stored it up in a little cart,
For my honey's heart.
Chorus

I BEG OF YOU

Words and Music by ROSE MARIE McCOY
and KELLY OWENS

please don't break my heart, I beg of you. ___ I don't
please don't say good - bye, I beg of you. ___

Hold my hand and prom-ise that you'll

al - ways love me true. Make me know you

(tacet)
love me the same way I love you, lit-tle girl. You

HOT DIGGITY
(Dog Ziggity Boom)

Words and Music by AL HOFFMAN
and DICK MANNING

HUSHABYE

Words and Music by DOC POMUS
and MORT SHUMAN

Hush - a - bye, hush - a - bye; oh, my dar - ling, don't you cry.
Guard - ian an - gels up a - bove, take care of the one I love.

Ooh, _____ ooh. _____

Pil - lows ly - ing on your bed; oh, my dar - ling, rest your head.
Sand - man will be com - ing soon, sing - ing you a slum - ber tune.

Ooh, _____ ooh. _____

I DON'T CARE IF THE SUN DON'T SHINE

Words and Music by
MACK DAVID

('Til)
I KISSED YOU

Words and Music by
DON EVERLY

Moderately

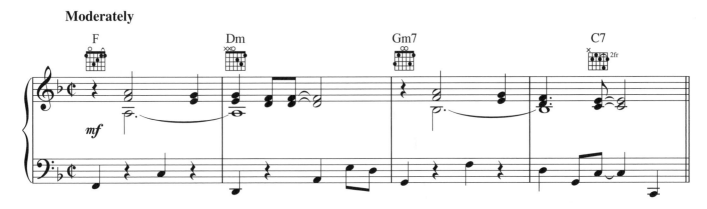

Nev - er felt like this __ un - til I kissed you.
Things have real - ly changed __ since I kissed you.

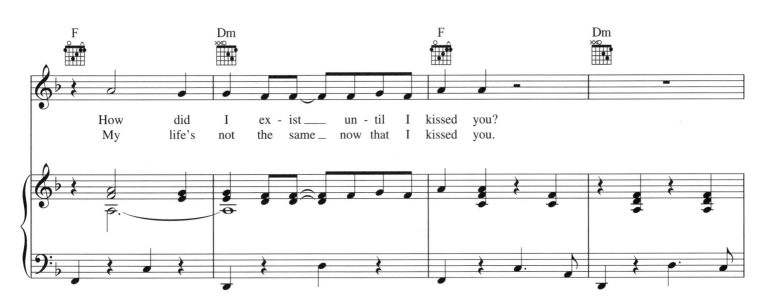

How did I ex - ist __ un - til I kissed you?
My life's not the same __ now that I kissed you.

I'M WALKING BEHIND YOU
(Look Over Your Shoulder)

Words and Music by
BILLY REID

Moderately slow

I'm walk-ing be-hind you _____ on your wed-ding day

and I'll hear you prom - ise _____ to love and o - bey.

Though you may for - get me, _____ you're still on my mind;

IN THE COOL, COOL, COOL OF THE EVENING

from the Paramount Picture HERE COMES THE GROOM

Words by JOHNNY MERCER
Music by HOAGY CARMICHAEL

IT'S ALMOST TOMORROW

Words and Music by WADE BUFF
and GENE ADKINSON

lips won't ___ be smil - ing, ___ your eyes will not shine, for
al - most ___ to - mor - row, ___ for here comes the sun, but

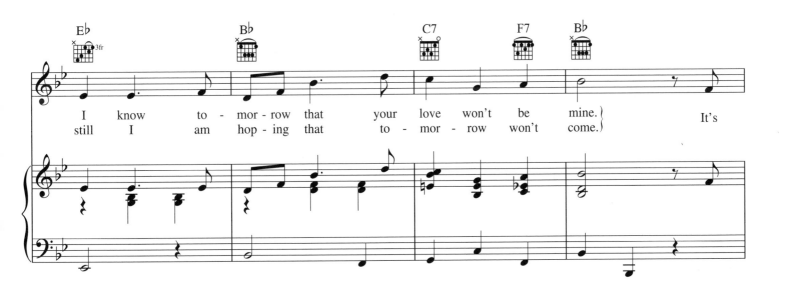

I know to - mor - row that your love won't be mine. }
still I am hop - ing that to - mor - row won't come. }
It's

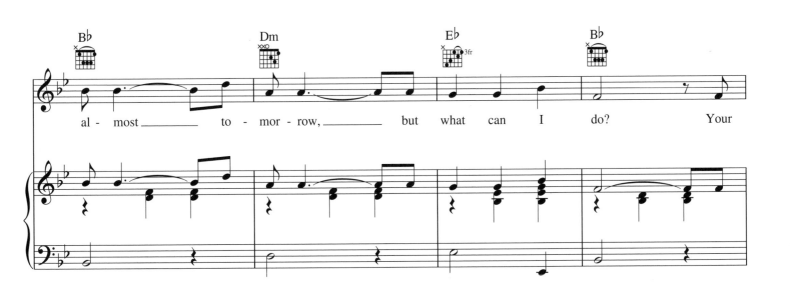

al - most ___ to - mor - row, ___ but what can I do? Your

kiss - es all tell me that your love is un - true. I'll love you _____ for-

ev - er _____ till stars cease to shine, and hope some - day,

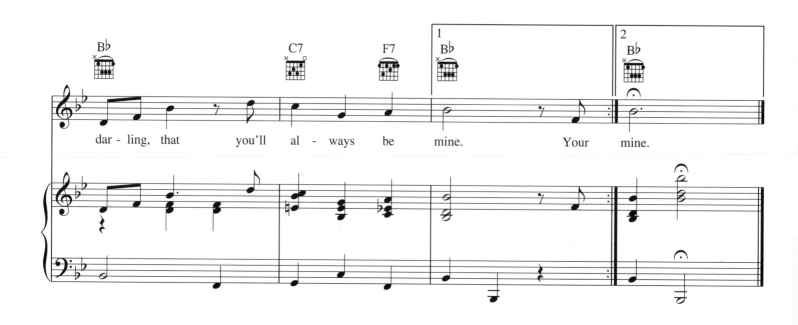

dar - ling, that you'll al - ways be mine. Your mine.

JAMBALAYA
(On the Bayou)

Words and Music by
HANK WILLIAMS

IT'S ONLY MAKE BELIEVE

Words and Music by CONWAY TWITTY
and JACK NANCE

IVORY TOWER

Words and Music by JACK FULTON
and LOIS STEELE

JUST IN TIME
from BELLS ARE RINGING

Words by BETTY COMDEN and ADOLPH GREEN
Music by JULE STYNE

KANSAS CITY

Words and Music by JERRY LEIBER
and MIKE STOLLER

Medium Blues

might take a train, _____ I might take a plane, _____ but
stay with that wom - an I know I'm gon - na die, _____ got - ta

if I have to walk _____ I'm goin' just the same. _____ I'm go - in' to)
find a brand - new ba - by and that's the rea - son why I'm go - in' to)

Kan - sas Cit - y, ___ Kan - sas Cit - y here I

come. _____ They got a

JUST WALKING IN THE RAIN

Words and Music by JOHNNY BRAGG
and ROBERT S. RILEY

KISSES SWEETER THAN WINE

Words by RONNIE GILBERT, LEE HAYS,
FRED HELLERMAN and PETE SEEGER
Music by HUDDIE LEDBETTER

Slowly, but with a steady beat

Verse

1. When I was a young man and nev-er been kissed, I got to

(Verses 2-5 see block lyric)

think-in' o-ver what I had missed. I got me a girl I

kissed her and then, Oh, Lord, I kissed her a-gain.

D.%. al Fine

Verse 2:
He asked me to marry and be his sweet wife,
And we would be so happy all of our life.
He begged and he pleaded like a natural man and then,
Oh, Lord, I gave him my hand. *(Repeat chorus)*

Verse 3:
I worked mighty hard and so did my wife,
A-workin' hand in hand to make a good life.
With corn in the fields and wheat in the bins and then,
Oh, Lord, I was the father of twins. *(Repeat chorus)*

Verse 4:
Our children numbered just about four
And they all had sweethearts knock on the door.
They all got married and they didn't wait, I was,
Oh, Lord, the grandfather of eight. *(Repeat chorus)*

Verse 5:
Now we are old and ready to go
We get to thinkin' what happened a long time ago.
We had lots of kids and trouble and pain, but,
Oh, Lord, we'd do it again. *(Repeat chorus)*

KO KO MO
(I Love You So)

Words and Music by EUNICE LEVY,
JAKE PORTER and FOREST WILSON

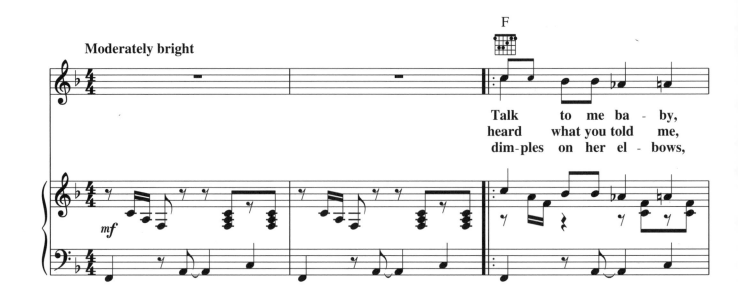

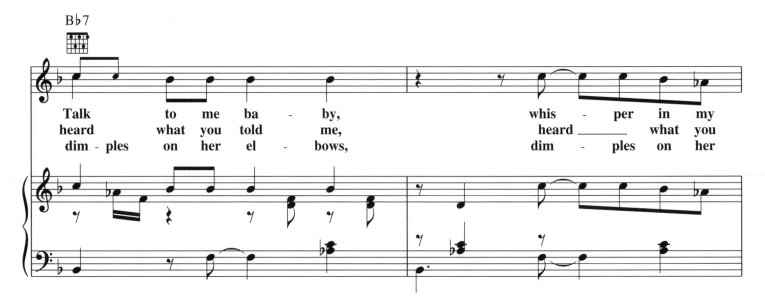

LA BAMBA

By RITCHIE VALENS

LIPSTICK ON YOUR COLLAR

Words by EDNA LEWIS
Music by GEORGE GOEHRING

LOLLIPOP

Words and Music by BEVERLY ROSS
and JULIUS DIXON

LONELY BOY

Words and Music by
PAUL ANKA

LONESOME TOWN

Words and Music by
BAKER KNIGHT

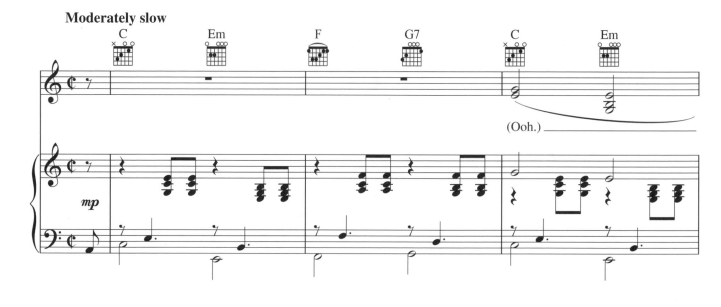

(Ooh.)

There's a place where lov-ers go ___ to cry their trou-bles a-

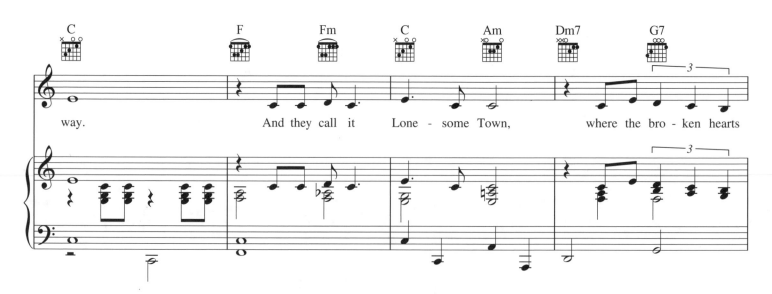

way. And they call it Lone-some Town, where the bro-ken hearts

LONG TALL SALLY

Words and Music by ENOTRIS JOHNSON,
RICHARD PENNIMAN and ROBERT BLACKWELL

Bright Rock

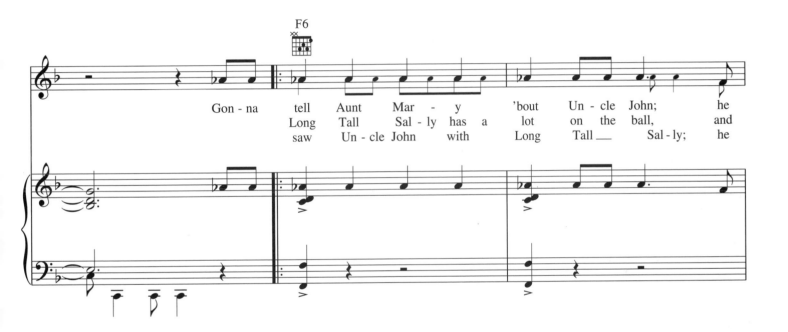

Gon - na tell Aunt Mar - y 'bout Un - cle John; he
Long Tall Sal - ly has a lot on the ball, and
saw Un - cle John with Long Tall ___ Sal - ly; he

says he has the blues, but he has a lot of fun. Oh,
no - bod - y cares if she's long ___ and ___ tall. Oh,
saw Aunt Mar - y com - in' and he ducked back in the al - ley. Oh,

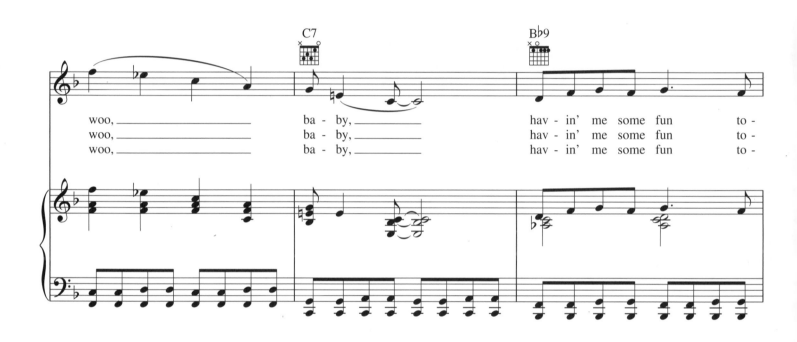

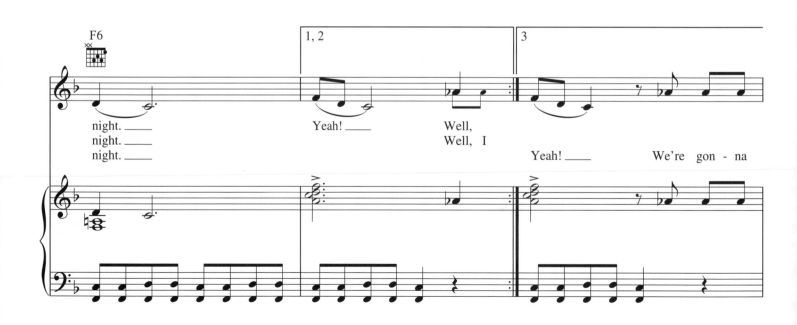

LOVE AND MARRIAGE

Words by SAMMY CAHN
Music by JAMES VAN HEUSEN

MAGIC MOMENTS

Lyric by HAL DAVID
Music by BURT BACHARACH

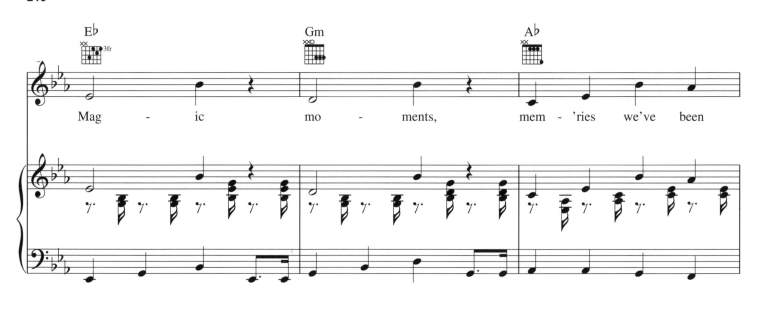

Mag - ic mo - ments, mem - 'ries we've been

shar - ing. Mag - ic mo - ments,

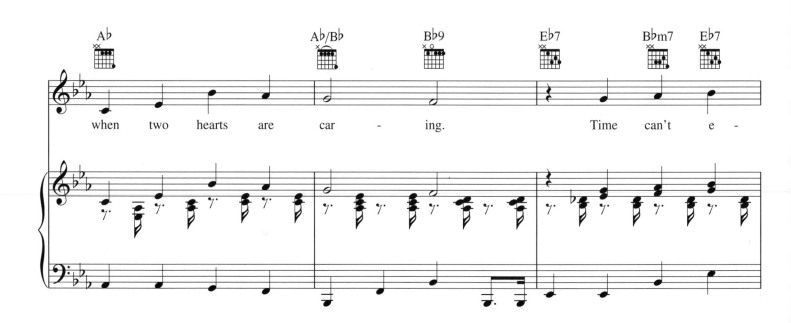

when two hearts are car - ing. Time can't e -

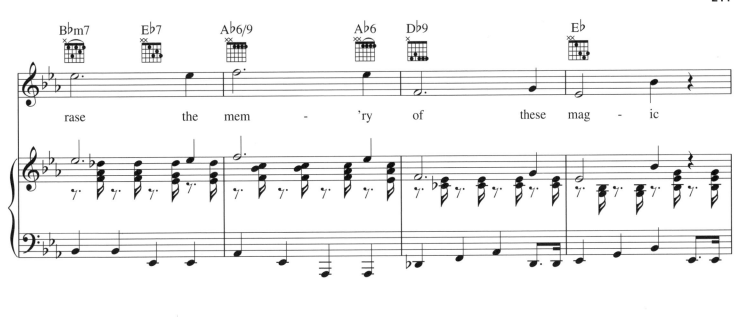

rase the mem - 'ry of these mag - ic

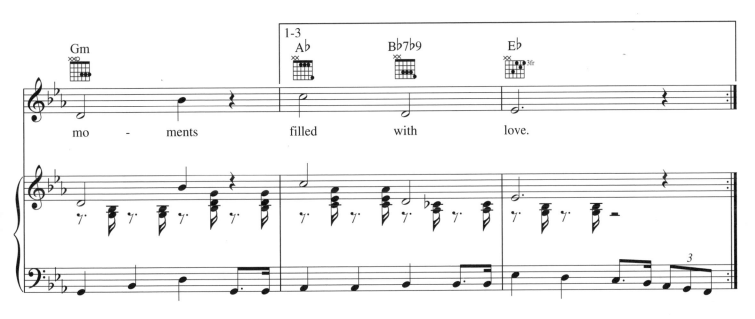

mo - ments filled with love.

filled with love.

LOVE ME TENDER

Words and Music by ELVIS PRESLEY
and VERA MATSON

A LOVER'S QUESTION

Words and Music by BROOK BENTON
and JIMMY WILLIAMS

Does she love me with all her heart?

Should I wor-ry when we're a-part?

A lov-er's ques-tion I'd like to know Oh,

LOVING YOU

Words and Music by JERRY LEIBER
and MIKE STOLLER

(You've Got)
THE MAGIC TOUCH

Words and Music by
BUCK RAM

MISTER SANDMAN

Lyric and Music by
PAT BALLARD

MEMORIES ARE MADE OF THIS

Words and Music by RICHARD DEHR,
FRANK MILLER and TERRY GILKYSON

MOMENTS TO REMEMBER

Words by AL STILLMAN
Music by ROBERT ALLEN

glad to share will e - cho thru the years. When
oth - er nights and oth - er days may find us gone our
sep - 'rate ways, We will have these mo - ments to re -
mem - ber. mem - ber.

MONA LISA

from the Paramount Picture CAPTAIN CAREY, U.S.A.

Words and Music by JAY LIVINGSTON
and RAY EVANS

(Put Another Nickel In)
MUSIC! MUSIC! MUSIC!

Words and Music by STEPHAN WEISS
and BERNIE BAUM

MY HEART CRIES FOR YOU

Music by PERCY FAITH
Lyrics by CARL SIGMAN

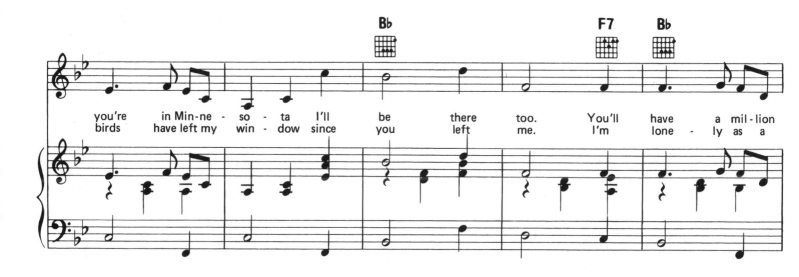

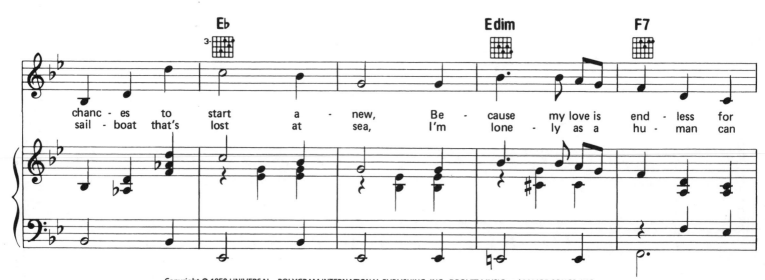

MY HEART IS AN OPEN BOOK

Lyric by HAL DAVID
Music by LEE POCKRISS

OH, LONESOME ME

Words and Music by
DON GIBSON

MY PRAYER

Music by GEORGES BOULANGER
Lyric and Musical Adaptation by JIMMY KENNEDY

NEVER BE ANYONE ELSE BUT YOU

Words and Music by
BAKER KNIGHT

OH! MY PA-PA
(O Mein Papa)

English Words by JOHN TURNER and GEOFFREY PARSONS
Music and Original Lyric by PAUL BURKHARD

PAPA LOVES MAMBO

Words and Music by AL HOFFMAN,
DICK MANNING and BIX REICHNER

PARTY DOLL

Words and Music by JIMMY BOWEN
and BUDDY KNOX

(You've Got)
PERSONALITY

Words and Music by LLOYD PRICE
and HAROLD LOGAN

PUT YOUR HEAD ON MY SHOULDER

Words and Music by
PAUL ANKA

Put your head on my should - er, Hold me in your arms, Ba - by.

Squeeze me oh so tight, Show me that you love me too. ___

___ Put your lips close to mine, dear. Won't you kiss me once, Ba - by?

POOR LITTLE FOOL

Words and Music by
SHARON SHEELEY

PRIMROSE LANE

Words and Music by WAYNE SHANKLIN
and GEORGE CALLENDER

ROCK AROUND THE CLOCK

Words and Music by MAX C. FREEDMAN
and JIMMY DeKNIGHT

SEA OF LOVE

Words and Music by GEORGE KHOURY
and PHILIP BAPTISTE

Medium slow Fifties Rock

SEARCHIN'

Words and Music by JERRY LEIBER
and MIKE STOLLER

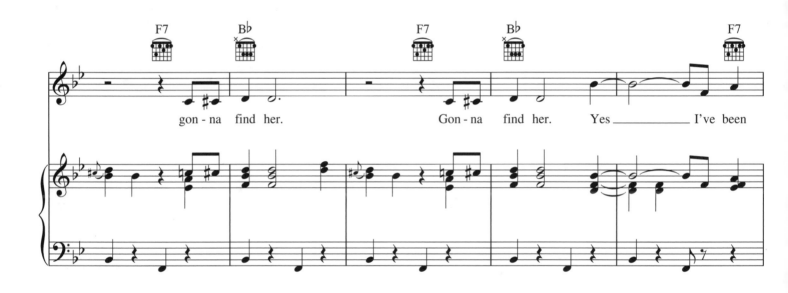

SEE SAW

Words and Music by STEVE CROPPER
and DON COVAY

Some-times you love me like a good man ought-a; Some-times you hurt me so bad _____ my tears run like wa - ter.

Your love __ is like a see - saw, go - in' up, down

all a - round __ like a see - saw. Some-times you

To Coda ⊕

tell me you're gon-na be __ my sweet can - dy man; __

Then, uh, some-times ba - by, don't know where I

SEE YOU LATER, ALLIGATOR

Words and Music by
ROBERT GUIDRY

SINCE I DON'T HAVE YOU

Words and Music by JAMES BEAUMONT,
JANET VOGEL, JOSEPH VERSCHAREN,
WALTER LESTER, LENNIE MARTIN,
JOSEPH ROCK and JOHN TAYLOR

SINCERELY

Words and Music by ALAN FREED
and HARVEY FUQUA

SINGING THE BLUES

Words and Music by
MELVIN ENDSLEY

SMOKE GETS IN YOUR EYES

from ROBERTA

Words by OTTO HARBACH
Music by JEROME KERN

SIXTEEN CANDLES

Words and Music by LUTHER DIXON
and ALLYSON R. KHENT

SIXTEEN TONS

Words and Music by
MERLE TRAVIS

Chorus

STAGGER LEE

Words and Music by LLOYD PRICE
and HAROLD LOGAN

TEACH ME TONIGHT

Words by SAMMY CAHN
Music by GENE DePAUL

THE STROLL

Words and Music by CLYDE OTIS
and NANCY LEE

stroll. _____ There's my love _____ stroll-ing in the door. __

____ There's my love _____ stroll-ing in the door. __

____ Ba-by, let's go stroll-ing by the can-dy

1
store.

2
store. _____

TAMMY

Words and Music by JAY LIVINGSTON
and RAY EVANS

Tears On My Pillow

Words and Music by SYLVESTER BRADFORD
and AL LEWIS

(Let Me Be Your)
TEDDY BEAR

Words and Music by KAL MANN
and BERNIE LOWE

Medium bright Rock

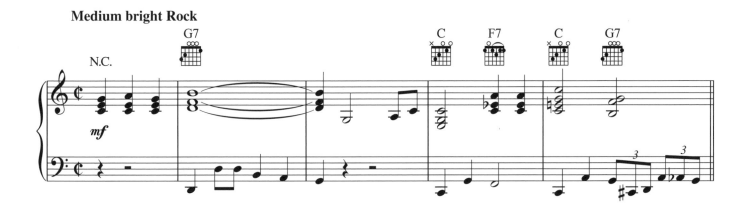

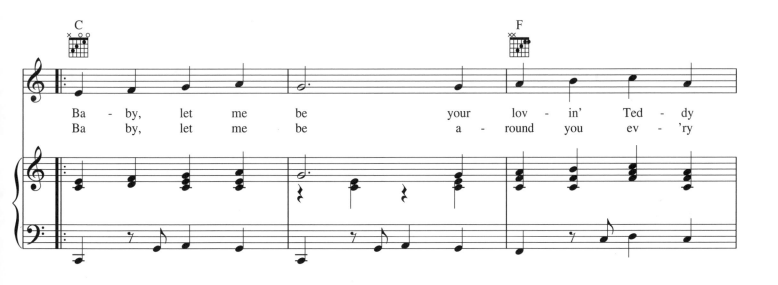

Ba - by, let me be   your lov - in' Ted - dy
Ba - by, let me be   a - round you ev - 'ry

Bear.   Put a chain a - round my neck ___   and
night.   Run your fin - gers through my hair ___   and

TENNESSEE WALTZ

Words and Music by REDD STEWART
and PEE WEE KING

TEQUILA

By CHUCK RIO

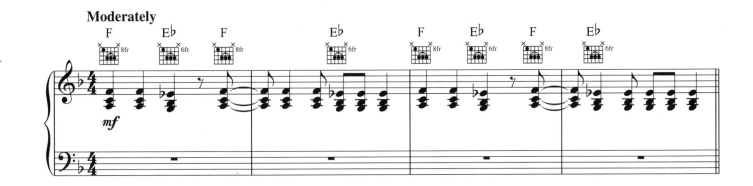

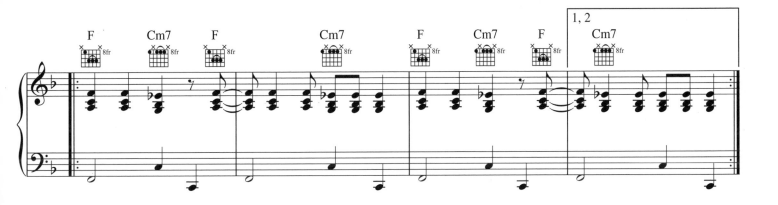

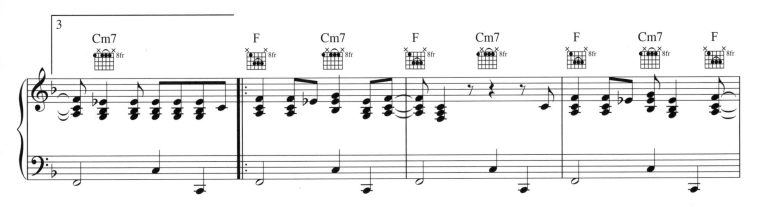

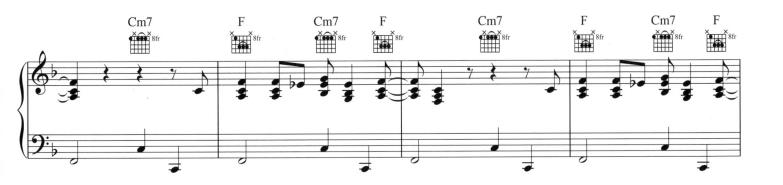

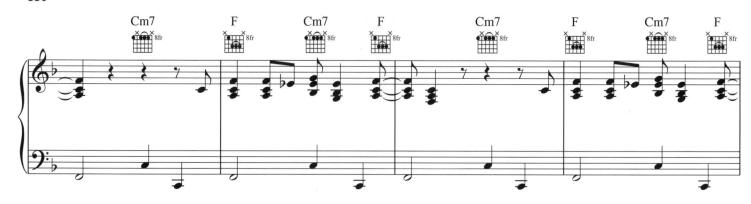

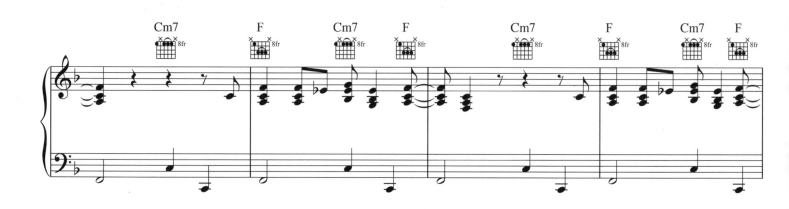

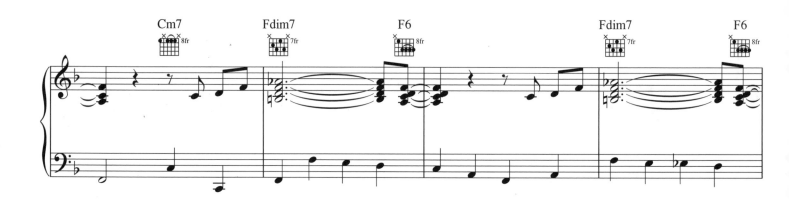

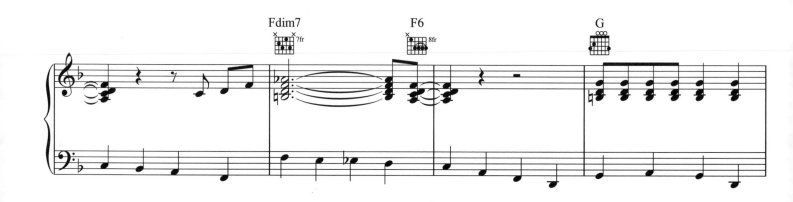

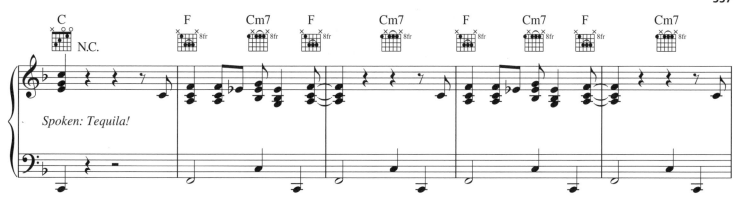

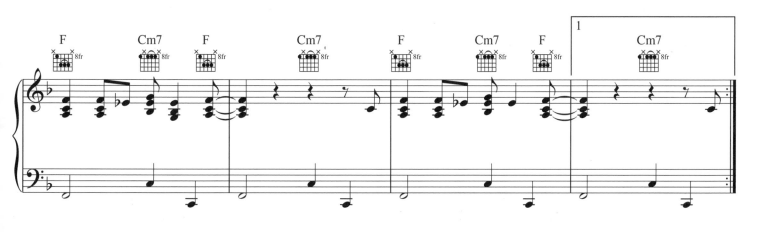

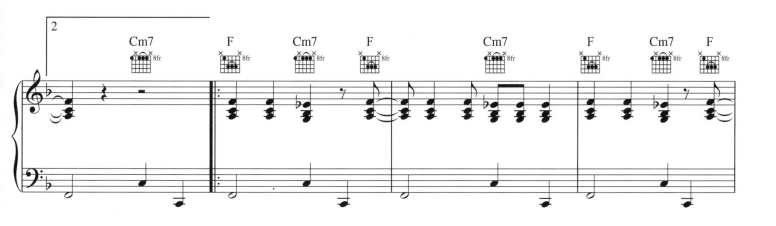

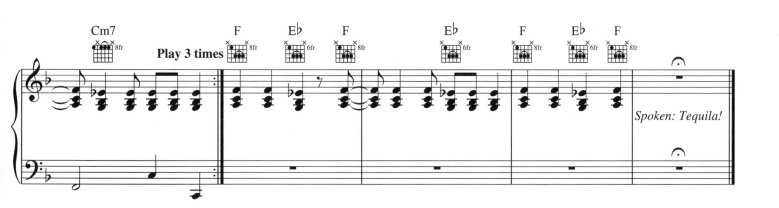

THAT'S AMORÉ
(That's Love)
from the Paramount Picture THE CADDY

Words by JACK BROOKS
Music by HARRY WARREN

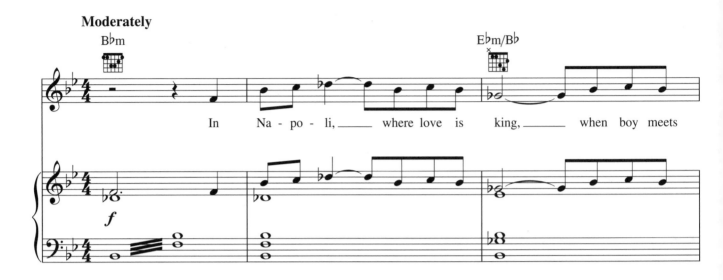

THERE GOES MY BABY

Words and Music by JERRY LEIBER,
MIKE STOLLER, BEN E. NELSON,
LOVER PATTERSON and GEORGE TREADWELL

TOM DOOLEY

Words and Music Collected, Adapted and Arranged by FRANK WARNER,
JOHN A. LOMAX and ALAN LOMAX
From the singing of FRANK PROFFITT

TONIGHT YOU BELONG TO ME

Words by BILLY ROSE
Music by LEE DAVID

TRUE LOVE

Words and Music by
COLE PORTER

TURN ME LOOSE

Words and Music by DOC POMUS
and MORT SHUMAN

THE WALK

Words and Music by
JIMMY McCRACKLIN

With a good beat

mf

Verse

Eb 6fr.

mp

1. Well,— I — know you heard of the Su - sie Q,   And
2. Well,—) I — know you heard of the Tex - as Hop,   And
3. Well,—) I — know you heard of the old mam - bo,   And
4. Now,—) if you don't —— know what it's all a - bout,   ——

Refrain

TWILIGHT TIME

Lyric by BUCK RAM
Music by MORTY NEVINS and AL NEVINS

THE WAYWARD WIND

Words and Music by HERB NEWMAN
and STAN LEBOWSKY

WEAR MY RING
AROUND YOUR NECK

Words and Music by BERT CARROLL
and RUSSELL MOODY

Bright tempo

Won't you wear my ring
ring up a - round your neck
up a - round your neck To tell the
To tell the

world I'm yours, by heck. Let them see
world I'm yours, by heck. Let them know

your love for me, _____ And let them see by the ring a - round your
I love you so, _____ And let them know by the ring a - round your

WHAT'D I SAY

Words and Music by
RAY CHARLES

A WHITE SPORT COAT
(And a Pink Carnation)

Words and Music by
MARTY ROBBINS

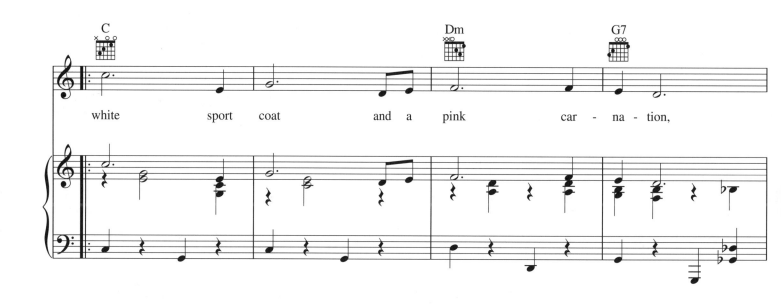

white   sport coat   and a   pink   car - na - tion,

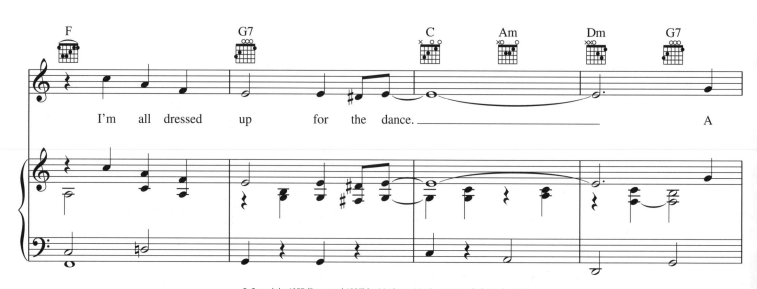

I'm all dressed up   for   the dance.

WHY

Words and Music by BOB MARCUCCI
and PETER DeANGELIS

WHY DON'T YOU BELIEVE ME

Words and Music by LEW DOUGLAS,
LUTHER KING LANEY and LEROY W. RODDE

YOU BELONG TO ME

Words and Music by PEE WEE KING,
REDD STEWART and CHILTON PRICE

YOUNG BLOOD

Words and Music by JERRY LEIBER,
MIKE STOLLER and DOC POMUS

I saw her stand - in' on the cor - ner,
I took one look and I was frac - tured.
I could - n't sleep a wink for try - in'.

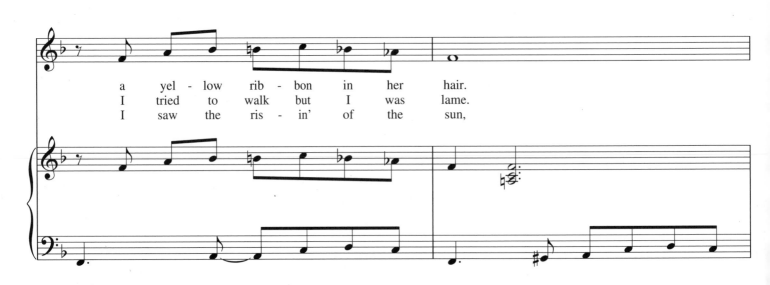

a yel - low rib - bon in her hair.
I tried to walk but I was lame.
I saw the ris - in' of the sun,

CODA

can't get you out-ta my mind. _____

Young blood, _ young blood, _

young blood, _ I

can't get you out-ta my mind. _____

WONDERFUL! WONDERFUL!

Words by BEN RALEIGH
Music by SHERMAN EDWARDS

Some-times we walk hand in hand by the sea and we breathe in the cool salt-y
Some-times we stand on the top of a hill and we gaze at the earth and the

air; you turn to me with a kiss in your eyes and my
sky; I turn to you and you melt in my arms, there we

heart feels a thrill be-yond com-pare! Then your lips cling to mine, it's
are, dar-ling, on-ly you and I! What a mo-ment to share, it's